Pebble® Plus

Cool Sports Facts

Cool Soccer Facts

by Abby Czeskleba

Consulting Editor: Gail Saunders-Smith, PhD

Consultant: Craig Coenen, PhD
Associate Professor of History
Mercer County Community College
West Windsor, New Jersey

CAPSTONE PRESS
a capstone imprint

Pebble Plus is published by Capstone Press,
1710 Roe Crest Drive, North Mankato, Minnesota 56003.
www.capstonepub.com

Books published by Capstone Press are manufactured with paper
containing at least 10 percent post-consumer waste.

Library of Congress Cataloging-in-Publication Data
Czeskleba, Abby.
  Cool soccer facts / by Abby Czeskleba.
      p. cm.—(Pebble plus. Cool sports facts)
  Includes bibliographical references and index.
  Summary: "Simple text and full-color photos illustrate facts about the rules, equipment, and records of soccer"—
Provided by publisher.
  ISBN 978-1-4296-4479-2 (library binding)
  ISBN 978-1-4296-7394-5 (paperback)
  1. Soccer—Miscellanea—Juvenile literature. I. Title. II. Series.

  GV943.25.C94 2011
  796.334—dc22   2009051412

Editorial Credits
Erika L. Shores, editor; Kyle Grenz, designer; Eric Gohl, media researcher; Eric Manske, production specialist

Photo Credits
AP Images, 15; Kevork Djansezian, 21; Tony Gutierrez, 19
Comstock Images, cover (soccer ball), back cover, 1
Dreamstime/Diademimages, 9
FIFA via Getty Images Inc./Joern Pollex, 7
Getty Images Inc./AFP/Matt Campbell, 11
MLS via Getty Images Inc./German Alegria, 17
Shutterstock/cjpdesigns, 5, 13; ostill, cover

Note to Parents and Teachers

The Cool Sports Facts series supports national social studies standards related to people, places,
and culture. This book describes and illustrates soccer. The images support early readers in
understanding the text. The repetition of words and phrases helps early readers learn new
words. This book also introduces early readers to subject-specific vocabulary words, which are
defined in the Glossary section. Early readers may need assistance to read some words and to
use the Table of Contents, Glossary, Read More, Internet Sites, and Index sections of the book.

Printed in the United States of America in North Mankato, Minnesota.
062012   006824R

Table of Contents

Goal! 4

Cool Equipment 6

Cool Rules 10

Cool Records 14

Glossary 22

Read More 23

Internet Sites 23

Index 24

Goal!

In the United States, it's called soccer. Nearly everywhere else, fans call it football. It's the world's most popular sport.

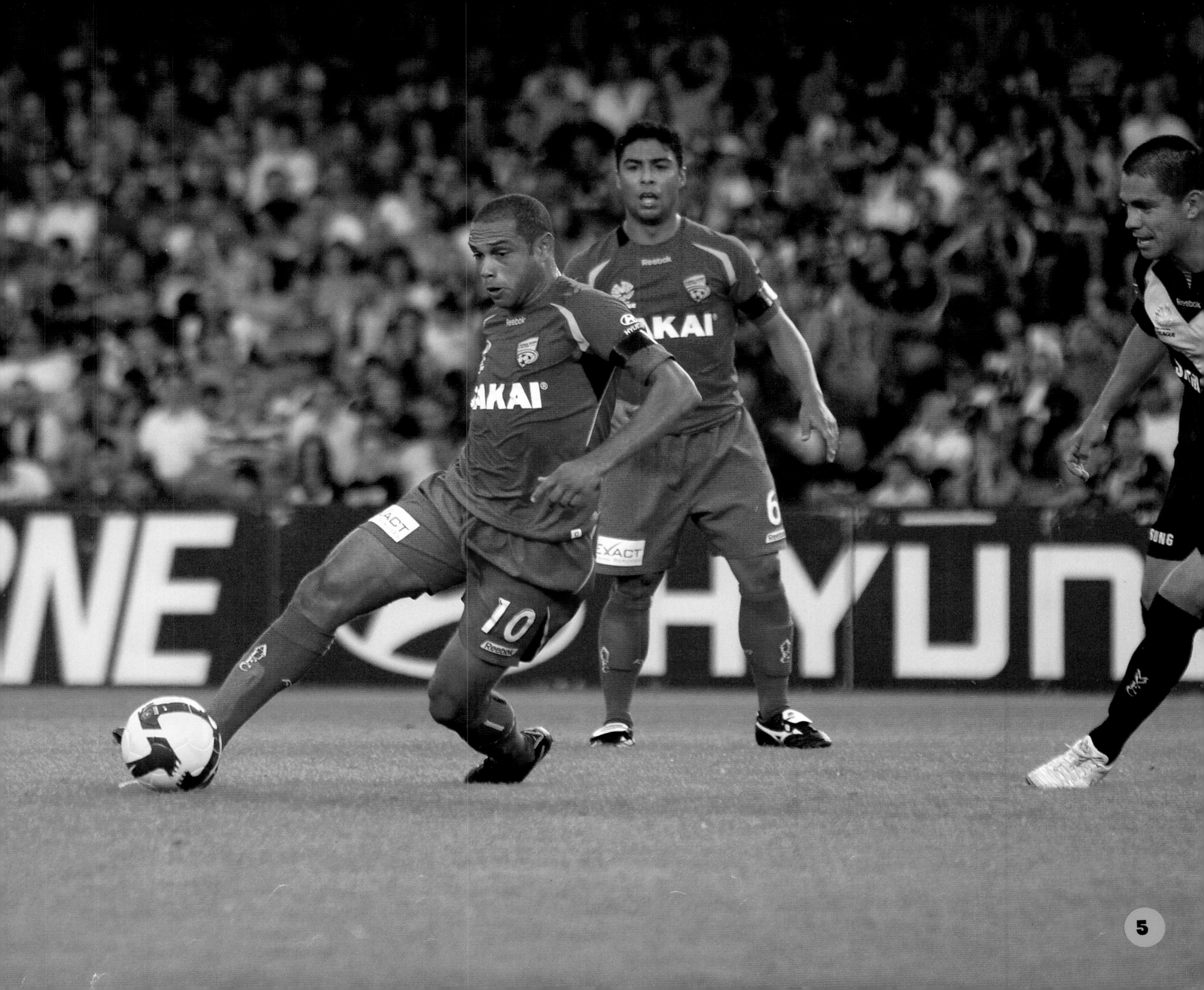

Cool Equipment

Adidas designs

a new soccer ball

for each World Cup.

The World Cup is played

every four years.

Soccer players wear shoes
called cleats.
The shoes grip the field
when the players run.

Cool Rules

Referees try to stay away from the soccer ball. If the ball hits a referee, play continues.

Players love to celebrate

scoring a goal.

But it's against the rules

to take off shirts to celebrate.

Cool Records

Pelé is a soccer legend.
He scored 1,281 goals
in his career. Pelé played
on three World Cup
championship teams.

15

The Los Angeles Galaxy

played in front of 93,137 fans

in August 2009.

It was the biggest U.S. crowd

for a non-World Cup game.

In 2002, Hakan Sükür scored a goal in the first 11 seconds of a game. It was the fastest goal in World Cup history.

Soccer star Mia Hamm scored

158 goals in world games.

She holds the record for

the most world game goals

by a male or female player.

Glossary

career—the experiences an athlete has playing a sport over time

celebrate—to do something fun for a special occasion

legend—someone who is among the best in what they do

popular—liked or enjoyed by many people

record—when something is done better than anyone has ever done it before

World Cup—a soccer tournament held every four years; 32 teams from around the world compete to win the World Cup championship

Read More

Armentrout, David, and Patricia Armentrout. *Mia Hamm.* Discover the Life of a Sports Star. Vero Beach, Fla.: Rourke, 2004.

Cline-Ransome, Lesa. *Young Pelé: Soccer's First Star.* New York: Schwartz & Wade Books, 2007.

Internet Sites

FactHound offers a safe, fun way to find Internet sites related to this book. All of the sites on FactHound have been researched by our staff.

Here's all you do:

Visit *www.facthound.com*

FactHound will fetch the best sites for you!

Index

Adidas, 6
balls, 6, 10
cleats, 8
goals, 12, 14, 18, 20
Hamm, Mia, 20
Los Angeles Galaxy, 16

Pelé, 14
referees, 10
rules, 10, 12
shirts, 12
Sükür, Hakan, 18
World Cup, 6, 14, 18

Word Count: 182
Grade: 1
Early-Intervention Level: 22